STAND FAST

DEBORAH BYKER-BENSON

STAND FAST
Copyright © 2025 by Deborah Byker-Benson

Other books by this author can be found at derbwerbster.com.

ISBN: 979-8-9926279-0-9 (softcover)
ISBN: 979-8-9926279-1-6 (Ebook)

Cover Artwork by Graham R. Allingham
Interior Design/Formatting by Vickie Swisher, Studio 20|20

DEDICATION

In memory of Rev. John J. Byker, 1924–2010

Many people speak of Reformation as a period of history, as a tradition, as a safe social construct, or as a well formulated and systematic summary of Biblical truth. My father also spoke and taught of reformation in those ways but more importantly he spoke of it by **walking the talk**. His heart was with God in Christ alone; it beat a rhythm of daily, progressive re-formation through self-examination and repentance as a response of love toward God and the neighbor (Matthew 22:36-40). His standards for re-formation were aimed toward the likeness of Jesus Christ (1 Peter 2:21). Of course my dad failed to meet the perfect and unyielding standard of Christ, just as we all do, but his stride toward Christ was easy and light (Matthew 11:27-30) because he rested only in the work of Christ (Acts 4:12) and never in his own works. Whatever the struggles between his old man of sin and the new man in Christ, my father's life exemplified the triumph of standing fast in Christ alone as "a light on a hill" (Matthew 5:14). As the firefly's glow is not worthy to be compared with the sun, so "the sufferings" and struggles of my fathers life "are not worthy to be compared with the glory which" has been "revealed" to and in him through Jesus Christ His Lord (Romans 8:18). May the same incomparable glory be revealed to and in all of us, the nine sons and daughters of Rev. John J. Byker, and also to our children from generation to generation.

PROLOGUE

This book has been written for my beloved children and grandchildren, nieces and nephews, and brothers and sisters in Christ. It has also been written for the ministry partners in Haiti, chosen of God to bear both the privilege and the heaviness of serving the Lord in unimaginably difficult circumstances.

To put it another way, the book was written for those that I love and to whom I have varying degrees of relational responsibility. That is, to those that did not have the indescribable blessing of being led to the Father, Son, and Spirit by the Grace of God's choosing, as sons and daughters of the earthly father, Rev. John J. Byker.

And if by God's will, may it be read by as many as the Lord in His grand design will cause to read it.

TABLE OF CONTENTS

PREFACE

A Sovereign Protector I have,
Unseen, yet forever at hand,
Unchangeably faithful to save,
Almighty to rule and command.

He smiles, and my comforts abound;
His grace as the dew shall descend;
And walls of salvation surround;
The soul He delights to defend.

Augustus Toplady, 1740–1778

CHAPTER 1

Why Stand Fast?

HEBREWS 2:1-4

*"For this reason we must pay much closer attention
to what we have heard, so that we do not drift away from it.
For if the word spoken through angels proved unalterable,
and every violation and act of disobedience received
a just punishment, **how will we escape if we neglect
so great a salvation?** After it was at first spoken
through the Lord, it was confirmed to us by those who heard,
God also testifying with them, both by signs and wonders,
and by various miracles and by gifts
of the Holy Spirit according to His own will."*

The Bible passages referenced in footnotes throughout this book, unless otherwise noted, are from the New American Standard Bible (NASB). I would urge you to read all the footnotes with the prayer and expectation that the Spirit will lead you, through the Word, and throughout life, "into all truth" (John 16:13).

This first chapter will briefly explore an influential thought-leader and his religion in order to answer the question, "why stand fast?" The ultimate and definitive definition of religion is "response to God, as He reveals Himself in His creation, and in His Holy Word." Although libraries are filled with the writings of many different thought-leaders and their religions, I've chosen the example of the scientist Richard Dawkins and the religion materialism. Dawkins has been chosen because of the clarity of his response to God and materialism has been chosen because it is a particularly aggressive and demonic force behind the evil absurdities in contemporary life against which a believer in Jesus Christ must stand fast; but there are many others.

Richard Dawkins believes that all living creatures are bytes of digital information issuing forth from genetic material. To him, creatures are matter alone, existing for the sole purpose of carrying genetic material into the next attempt of DNA molecules to survive, replicate, and evolve to higher forms. Even consciousness and intelligence among humans are considered by Dawkins to be randomly colliding matter in the brain to produce the phantom we ignorantly (according to him) call the mind. In his book *The Selfish Gene* he belabors these and other "virtues" of matter in general and DNA in specific.[1]

In *The God Delusion* Dawkins belabors the "vices" of God, expostulating aggressively saying that "the God of the Old Testament is arguably the most unpleasant character in all fiction: jealous and proud of it; a petty, unjust, unforgiving control-freak; a vindictive, bloodthirsty ethnic cleanser; a misogynistic, homophobic, racist, infanticidal, genocidal, filicidal, pestilential, megalomaniacal, sadomasochistic, capriciously malevolent bully."[2] The real delusion for Dawkins is his assumption that he has no

---

1   (Dawkins, 1976)
2   (Dawkins, 2006)

god.[3] Like all the rest of us, Dawkins has *Gotta Serve Somebody*.[4]

How could any being, whether real or fictitious, be unpleasant to a materialist if the standard of measure is the replication and evolution of DNA? According to Dawkins, his thoughts are random collisions in the phantom of his mind to serve replication and evolution of DNA. There is, according to him, nothing else outside the random collision of molecules to replicate and evolve DNA. Therefore DNA is the only absolute against which to measure "right" or "wrong." The only pleasant (or righteous) creatures would be those that reproduce early, often, and well, while the only unpleasant (or unrighteous) creatures would be those that reproduce slowly, poorly, or not at all. Whatever else creatures do is irrelevant. "The man doth protest **too** much, methinks,"[5] perhaps as a result of **megalomania.**

Is Dawkins in fact as unpleasant as he accuses God of being? On one occasion he suggested that a woman "abort it and try again" because the fetus she carried had Downs Syndrome. He said it would be immoral not to do so.[6] Dawkins is **capricious** in advising **filicide** on the basis of god-like DNA. According to him, morality is established by supporting the evolution of DNA more efficiently or effectively. This is also the basis of his justification for supporting the legal **infanticide** erroneously called abortion and "women's health." Dawkins concludes that which is right or wrong according to his assumptions about the apparently "mindful purposes" of DNA to evolve to higher forms. His "morality" for women is **misogynistic.** If he were

---

3   Romans 1:25 "For they exchanged the truth of God for a lie, and worshiped and served the creature rather than the Creator, who is blessed forever. Amen."

4   (Dylan, 1979)

5   Shakespeare, Hamlet, Act III, Scene II.

6   https://www.theguardian.com/science/2014/aug/21/richard-dawkins-immoral-not-to-abort-a-downs-syndrome-foetus

to decide by his experimentation that an ethnicity, life-style, or nation were thwarting, or not progressing, the evolution of DNA toward superior forms of life would he support **ethnic cleansing, homophobia or genocide?** Obviously he would in just the same way he justifies the "morality" of filicide and infanticide.

Dawkins further asserts that non-matter cannot exist because there is no experiment to prove non-matter. Equally true is the statement that **chance alone** cannot exist because there is no experiment to prove the absence of other possibilities such as a force[7] operating above or outside matter and random chance. **Chance alone**, according to Dawkins' materialism, cannot exist. God doesn't require an experiment; He requires humility and Dawkins' religion speaks against other religions with the pride of a **malevolent bully.**

In another well-circulated quote Dawkins' says, "Faith is the great cop-out, the great excuse to evade the need to think and evaluate evidence. Faith is the belief in spite of, even perhaps because of, the lack of evidence."[8] He further says that there is no rational proof for God, miracles, or the soul. Has Dawkins copped-out by failing to evaluate that his blind faith in genetic material and chance alone cannot be proved or disproved by experimentation?

Has Dawkins copped-out when pitting faith against reason as if they cannot co-exist? Has he ignored the abundance of evidence that faith and reason have co-existed, among material beings, throughout all of recorded history? Dawkins suggests unequivocally that **only** matter and scientific reason are valid considerations and that beliefs in any matter-transcending force

---

7   Proverbs 16:33 "The lot is cast into the lap, but its every decision is from the Lord." Colossians 1:17 "He is before all things, and in Him all things hold together."

8   (Dawkins, 2006)

are **only** unreasonable and reactive. Many reasonable and non-reactive scientists, like Pascal, Mendel, Newton, Galilei, Boyle, and Copernicus to name a few, believed in the one God, or minimally in matter-transcending forces.

Science is not the only route to knowledge as Dawkins suggests. Science is the only route to knowledge about the function and properties of matter that the senses can detect. That does not prove or disprove, nor can it, the existence of forces that transcend matter. Dawkins' either-or argument sounds like the defensiveness of an **unforgiving control-freak**, unable and unwilling to value or examine anything outside of his own assumptions.

The overconfident statement that "God is unnecessary. Science can explain Nature without any help from supernatural causes like God"[9] is euphemistic for belief **in** science **as** god rather than belief in God. Perhaps Dawkins has failed to evaluate that science cannot experiment on the origin, self-generation, or chance-only collisions of matter. Evolution and the Big Bang for example, have been reverse engineered from experimentation and observation of matter that exists, in order to exclude the only other option. Namely, that there is a force outside and above matter. That is, outside the religion of materialism under the leadership of scientists playing god.

Dawkins said that "The universe is a complex machine whose workings are steadily being demystified by science. Any other way of viewing the world is superstitious and reactionary."[10] If those with "god delusions" are superstitious and reactionary Dawkins is the pot calling the kettle black. Materialists simply react (respond) to the idea of a God that isn't themselves and their superstition

---

9   (Dawkins, 2006)
10   (Dawkins, The God Delusion, 2006)

extends to the unproved, reverse engineered theories they assume. "Superstitious and reactionary" seems like a **petty and unjust** indictment against those humble enough to consider that there may be a force higher than themselves.

The universe **is** complex and Dawkins believes it is a machine made up of solid matter randomly colliding to haphazardly form more and more complex objects until over the course of billions of years the random collisions produced life and eventually human life. Conveniently, Dawkins avoids the question of the origin of the first "solid matter" that was "randomly colliding."

What **is** evident about matter by simple observation and any experimentation at all is that there is enormous design, complexity, organization and interconnectedness everywhere in the matter that makes up the universe. That evidence alone suggests a transcendent force far more elegantly than the clumsy, crude mechanism of self-generation and random chance. The religion of materialism is at least as strongly superstitious and reactionary as is the belief in a force or power above and beyond what Dawkins believes in: self-generation of matter, and the formation of enormous design, complexity, organization and interconnectedness throughout the vast universe by random chance alone.

Dawkins ridicules the notion of God as Creator by saying that "such a God didn't need to create the cosmos through the Big Bang and billions of years of evolution. Such a God could have created it whole and perfect to begin with."[11] Has Dawkins **read** the Bible? "Whole and perfect to begin with" is exactly what God said He did.[12] It was scientists observing matter **while rejecting or ignoring God's revelation** that reverse engineered to theories like

---

11   (Dawkins, 2006)

12   Genesis 1, and concluding with Genesis 1:31 "God saw all that he had made, and behold, it was very good."

the Big Bang or the self-generation and evolution of all things by chance. The evidence found in matter suggests more strongly that the earth was created "whole and perfect" and that it is currently devolving than that it was randomly self-generated and evolving toward perfection through again, random collisions of matter.

A believer in the one God of the Old Testament, who has studied the full revelation might say, "I see that design, complexity, organization and interconnectedness exists; let me give thanks for it, study it, figure out how it works, and use it for God's glory and the good of mankind." This approach assumes that an objective observation of the world of matter, as a conscious, intelligent, learning being, is a privilege in service to a force and power that transcends matter and themselves; it's a humble approach.[13]

Alternatively, a materialist might say in effect, "I see the design, complexity, organization and interconnectedness and I'm going to ignore it in my studies of matter because I've decided it's all the byproduct of self-generation and random chance. Therefore, I say what is right or wrong for humanity and I decide what is good or bad for mankind as a disciple of the god of science." This approach assumes that an objective observation of the world of matter entitles the observer to play God; it's an exceptionally prideful approach.[14]

Dawkins' quote about the unpleasantness of the God of the Old Testament conveniently ignores most of the Old and New Testament. It is necessary as a materialist to reduce God's magnificent revelation of Himself to an unpleasant fictional character in order to perpetuate the imaginary narrative that he can serve the god of science and/or self. Dawkins, materialists,

---

13   Proverbs 11:2b "but with humility comes wisdom."
14   Proverbs 16:18 "Pride goes before destruction, and a haughty spirit before stumbling."

science, and scientists are not the only ones that perpetuate imaginary narratives in response to God's revelation; we all do.

God has self-revealed in a literary miracle of astounding breadth and depth, which He authored and has preserved over millennia, in a Word that "endures forever" (Isaiah 40:6-8). Dawkins **unjustly** misrepresents what God has said in His Word. If Dawkins' book rights were misrepresented he could seek justice based on God's law, but could not seek justice on the basis of his own religion. Dawkins' right to defend his book rights from misrepresentation is derived from the absolute law elucidated in God's book when He states, "you shall not bear false witness against your neighbor (Exodus 20:16)." Dawkins is justified in defending his book rights while He unjustly misrepresents God's.

Dawkins is not responding to God in rejection because of a lack of evidence.[15] He responds with rejection because following the "whole and perfect" creation, humanity fell into sin and has inherited from Adam an opposition to God and His law in favor of self as god, or self-made gods. Additionally, from that nature, each human walks willfully in opposition to God's revealed

---

15   Romans 1:19-20 "because that which is known about God is evident within them; for God made it evident to them. For since the creation of the world His invisible attributes, His eternal power and divine nature, have been clearly seen, being understood through what has been made, so that they are without excuse."; Psalm 19:1-2 "The heavens are telling of the glory of God; and their expanse is declaring the work of His hands. Day to day pours forth speech, and night to night reveals knowledge."

rights[16] as Creator,[17] Law-giver,[18] and Judge.[19] We are all initially responding against God because we'd rather **be** God than **serve** God. Dawkins is like all of us, although he is more publicly angry and belligerent while most of us hide and blame-shift.

Dawkins' quote about God is actually an incomplete articulation of the characteristics exhibited by Dawkins and all other humans, to some degree, throughout all of history. God's character on the other hand, if His Word is not misrepresented, is complete, perfect, unchanging and sovereign.

If only God had communicated all that is necessary to live and die happily to spend eternity in fellowship with Him. **If only** God had revealed a Way to escape the consequences of breaking His law.[20] **If only** God had revealed a way to atone for righteousness left undone.[21] **If only** God had revealed a Way to be cleared in the court of absolute law.[22] **If only** God had revealed a Way to finally and eternally escape all of humanities (**and my own**) pettiness; injustice; grudge-bearing; control mongering;

---

16   Job 41:11 "Who has preceded Me, that I should pay him? Everything under heaven is Mine." (*NIV*)

17   Genesis 1:1 "In the beginning, God created the heavens and the earth."

18   Matthew 5:17-19 "Do not presume that I came to abolish the Law or the Prophets; I did not come to abolish, but to fulfill. For truly I say to you, until heaven and earth pass away, not the smallest letter or stroke of a letter shall pass from the Law, until all is accomplished! Therefore, whoever nullifies one of the least of these commandments, and teaches others to do the same, shall be called least in the kingdom of heaven; but whoever keeps and teaches them, he shall be called great in the kingdom of heaven;" see also Exodus 20:1-17

19   Isaiah 33:22 "For the Lord is our judge, the Lord is our lawgiver, the Lord is our king; He will save us."

20   John 3:16 "For God so loved the world, that He gave His only Son, so that everyone who believes in Him will not perish but have eternal life."

21   Romans 3:21-22 "But now apart from the Law the righteousness of God has been revealed, being witnessed by the Law and the Prophets, but it is the righteousness of God through faith in Jesus Christ for all those who believe; for there is no distinction."

22   Matthew 26:28 "for this is My blood of the covenant, which is being poured out for many for forgiveness of sins."

pay-backs; bloodthirst; bigotry; misogyny; homophobia; racism; infanticide; genocide; filicide; pestilentialism; megalomania; sadomasochism; capriciousness; and all malevolent bullying of self and others, in thought, word or deed.[23] **If only**[24] the blind could see.

If not for the Grace of God and Faith (a gift) in Jesus Christ,[25] God's Word of Truth,[26] Christ's work alone,[27] and for the sake of God's glory[28] and our good,[29] we would all grope around in blindness while standing in the glorious light of God's revelation just as Dawkins does.[30]

Why should we stand fast? For many reasons but one prominent reason among them is so that we do not neglect the undeserved privilege of having received sight with respect to "so great a salvation (Hebrews 2:3)."

---

23 1 John 1:8 "If we say that we have no sin, we are deceiving ourselves and the truth is not in us."

24 Deuteronomy 32:29 "If only they were wise and they understood this; If only they would discern their future!"

25 Ephesians 2:8-9 "For by grace you have been saved through faith; and this is not of yourselves, it is the gift of God; not a result of works, so that no one may boast."

26 John 17:17 "Sanctify them in the truth; Your word is truth."; John 1:14a "And the Word became flesh and dwelt among us…" (*NKJV*).

27 Acts 4:12 "And there is salvation in no one else; for there is no other name under heaven that has been given among mankind by which we must be saved.

28 Ephesians 1:11-12 "In Him we also have obtained an inheritance, having been predestined according to the purpose of Him who works all things in accordance with the plan of His will, to the end that we who were the first to hope in the Christ would be to the praise of His glory.;" John 17:24 "Father, I desire that they also, whom You have given Me, be with Me where I am, so that they may see My glory which You have given Me, for You loved Me before the foundation of the world."

29 Romans 8:28 "And we know that God causes all things to work together for good to those who love God, to those who are called according to His purpose."

30 Romans 1:22 "Professing to be wise, they became fools." (*NKJV*) See also Romans 1:20 32.

CHAPTER 2

Self-Examine

1 CORINTHIANS 16:13-14

"Watch, stand fast in the faith, be brave, be strong.
Act like grown-ups. Let all you do be done with love
(toward God and the neighbor)."
(paraphrase)

Christians fluctuate between accepting risks to be obedient to God and expediently denying risks. This is the case because within fallen image-bearers of God, fear and guilt fight for supremacy over the love and trust commanded by God. That battle results in many forms of control and management rather than trust and obedience all throughout life.[31] To become more obedient and less expedient one must engage in the practice of self-examination.[32] Using the time period of Covid-19 as a case study, my dear ones, I urge self-examination of what it means to stand fast, (i.e.

---

31   Romans 7:19 "For the good that I want, I do not do, but I practice the very evil that I do not want."

32   2 Corinthians 13:5 "Test and evaluate yourselves to see whether you are in the faith and living your lives as [committed] believers. Examine yourselves [not me]! Or do you not recognize this about yourselves [by an ongoing experience] that Jesus Christ is in you—unless indeed you fail the test and are rejected as counterfeit?" (AMP)

obedient rather than expedient). Was compliance during that time obedience to God's command to obey the authorities? Or was 'obey the authorities' an expedient euphemism to avoid risk or save face in a tidal wave of groupthink?

Powerful reactive and emotive initiators of the flesh abounded during the period of Covid-19. The phrase "it's for your safety" was spoken like a broken record in the most nauseating display of disingenuous virtue signaling I've personally witnessed in all my life. That one phrase manipulated inordinate fears of illness and death, and inappropriate guilt (or pride) about failing (or believing to have succeeded) in controlling and managing a virus through isolation and self-protection. Interestingly, forms of that phrase have been used successfully in other dark periods of history to isolate, crush, and control populations.

Was it actually for our safety? **Were** we to be personally responsible for control and management of disease? Or was it that "the despotisms," "the powers," "the master spirits who are the world rulers of this present darkness," and/or "the spiritual forces of wickedness in the heavenly (supernatural) sphere,"[33] hard at work to isolate, crush and control? Whatever has happened, or will happen, as a result of the extremities of that time period, and regardless of the lie that our safety is in the hands of anyone other

---

33 Ephesians 6:12-14 "For we are not wrestling with flesh and blood [contending only with physical opponents], but against the despotisms, against the powers, against [the master spirits who are] the world rulers of this present darkness, against the spirit forces of wickedness in the heavenly (supernatural) sphere. Therefore put on God's complete armor, that you may be able to resist *and* stand your ground on the evil day [of danger], and, having done all [the crisis demands], to stand [firmly in your place]. Stand therefore [hold your ground], having tightened the belt of truth around your loins and having put on the breastplate of integrity *and* of moral rectitude and right standing with God." (*AMPC*).

than God, He laughs[34] at the kings and kingdoms of the world.

But did God witness, at that time, the body of Christ as a whole capitulate rather than stand fast, acting as a catalyst to the rise of evil rather than as a preservative of Truth? Did the church as a whole on earth demonstrate more fear of things that kill the body or of that which kills the soul ?[35]

As individual parts of the body of Christ, persons may be led by the spirit of God and unique circumstances, **as opposed to being led by anything else**, to determine actions that are different one from another. The question is whether we as individuals **have** self-examined in order to determine the **motivators** of our decisions and actions? If the church as a whole capitulated to something other than what God enjoins in His Word, is it safe to assume that the majority of the parts capitulated?

---

34   Psalm 2:1-4 "Why are the nations restless, and the peoples plotting in vain? The kings of the earth take their stand, and the rulers conspire together against the Lord and against His Anointed, saying, "Let's tear their shackles apart and throw their ropes away from us!" He who sits in the heavens laughs, the Lord scoffs at them."

35   Matthew 10:28 "And do not be afraid of those who kill the body but are unable to kill the soul; but rather fear Him who is able to destroy both soul and body in hell."

CHAPTER 3

Assemble

ACTS 5:29B

During the Covid-19 period,
authorities forbade churches to assemble for worship.
In Acts, when forbidden to do something God enjoins
(teach and preach), Peter and the other apostles said:
"We must obey God rather than men."

In 1854 during a plague of Asiatic cholera, Pastor Charles Spurgeon vowed to leave ministry work in London. Soon after that he was convicted by the Spirit that he must stay in London to continue his ministry. Spurgeon did not contract Asiatic cholera.[36] If he had, it would have been in the course of being obedient to God, in God's appointed time.[37]

God enjoins that we not forsake "the assembling of ourselves together...and so much the more as you see the Day

---

36   (The Spurgeon Center for Biblical Preaching at Midwestern Seminary, 2020)

37   Job 14:5 "Since his days are determined, the number of his months is with You; and You have set his limits so that he cannot pass."

approaching."[38] "The Day" is still "approaching," so why had the vast majority of church leaders forsaken assembling during the period of Covid-19? If the definition of "assembly" is to gather together in one place for a common purpose, were online services an expedient re-definition of the word "assembly"? And if not to avoid some kind of risk, whether real or perceived, then why?

Corporate worship (assembling) is a positive injunction given to the leaders of the Church. On that basis, Church leaders have arranged and provided for assembly all throughout church history.[39] Some, if necessary, in caves, forests, garages, fields, barns, and in a wide variety of dangers including but not limited to physical illness, public shame, and death by martyrdom.[40]

In fact, the dangers encountered throughout church history, under which leaders of churches have continued to assemble, are mostly far greater dangers than those of Covid-19 itself or reprisals of the then executive orders. It is for these obedient decisions that many throughout history have suffered and died. In some cases suffering and death was a sacrifice made intentionally for the purpose of preserving the freedom to assemble in worship for generations hence. In all cases though, it was for obedience and not because it was expedient.

There is legitimacy to the statement, as was easily and frequently bandied about in order to justify the cessation of assembly, that worship includes many forms other than assembly. The fact is though, that neither private worship, nor any other forms of worship are the point at issue. Corporate worship,

---

38   Hebrews 10:25 "not forsaking the assembling of ourselves together, as is the manner of some, but exhorting one another, and so much the more as you see the Day approaching." (*NKJV*)

39   Hebrews 11, read the full chapter.

40   (Foxe, 1978)

a positive injunction of God to church leaders to provide for assembly, is the point at issue in this chapter.

Very few churches continued to provide for assembly in worship throughout the period of Covid-19. Individuals made decisions, hopefully based on their own conscience and the leading of God in their unique circumstances, to attend those churches in person (or not). The question in this chapter though is about **corporate** worship. Was the cessation of assembly an abysmal failure of church leaders to lead God's people in standing fast? And did the people of God acquiesce easily, failing to say as Elijah did to an errant leader of Israel, "you have abandoned the Lord's commands and have followed the Baals."[41]

---

41   1 Kings 18:17-24 "When he saw Elijah, he said to him (Ahab), "Is that you, you troubler of Israel?" "I have not made trouble for Israel," Elijah replied. "But you and your father's family have. You have abandoned the Lord's commands and have followed the Baals." (*NIV*)

CHAPTER 4

Visit and Help

MATTHEW 25:39-40

"And when did we see You sick, or in prison,
and come to You?' And the King will answer
and say to them, 'Truly I say to you,
to the extent that you did it for one of the least
of these brothers or sisters of Mine,
you did it for Me.'"

Lord Craven was preparing to leave London during the Black Plague when he overheard a man say, "Lord Craven's leave of London to avoid the plague must mean his God lives in the country and not in the town."[42] Subsequently, Lord Craven was convicted by God's words, "...surely He will deliver you...from the perilous pestilence,"[43] to stay in London.

Although most other noblemen left London for their country homes, Lord Craven stayed to visit and help the sick, donate land for burials, and advocate for quarantine of those infected as

---

42   (Roberts, 1980)

43   Psalm 91:3 "Surely He shall deliver you from the snare of the fowler and from the perilous pestilence." (*NKJV*)

opposed to isolation of the entire well population. I don't know about Lord Craven's heart toward God, but I know that if he erred in this case, he erred on the side of God's instruction. As it turns out, Lord Craven didn't die during the plague but if he had, and if he was at peace with God, he would have gone Home in the course of obedience to God, at the appointed time.[44]

Collective and systematic isolation and self-protection, rather than visiting and helping the sick and needy, is not a legitimate response of Christ followers that are physically well. In the period of Covid-19 though, collective and systematic isolation and self-protection was exactly the response of the church body of Christians as a whole. Remember, individual decisions according to God's leading are not the issue. I'm asking each individual follower of Christ to examine whether collective capitulation to evade God's then risky injunction to visit and help, **while physically well**, was obedient or expedient?

In the liberty with which Christ has set His people free,[45] and with the Spirit's leading, should Christians have made intentional efforts to visit the sick and help those struggling with Covid-19? And/or should they have visited and helped all those suffering the arguably more serious challenges that arose as a result of an isolated and self-protected world population?

Is freedom in Christ only about **what** one decides or is it also and more integrally **that** one decides in the exercise of liberty in Christ and not in fear of, well, anything else? Will the body of Christ collectively and systematically stand fast in the next authoritative orders that come in opposition to what God enjoins? Will you?

---

44 Ecclesiastes 3:2a "A time to give birth and a time to die."
45 Galatians 5:1 "It was for freedom that Christ set us free; therefore keep standing firm and do not be subject again to a yoke of slavery."

Perhaps Lord Craven realized that faith runs toward Refuge and not away from pestilence because ultimately, Christ is the refuge and hell the deadly pestilence. Have we?

CHAPTER 5

Take Shelter

PSALM 118:8

*"It is better to take shelter with the Lord
than to trust in man."*

As a result of personal self-examination during and after the time period of Covid-19, I realized that I was battling a disease more deadly than any virus, and even more dangerous than the heart-breaking and excessive collateral damage that resulted from reactions to the Covid-19 virus all around the world.

I battled against dominating anger[46] about the willing re-definition of the word "assemble"; the sharp rise of thought police; the widespread lack of spiritual (and rational) thought; the willing participation of Christians in the acceleration of (already) declining civil and religious liberty; the widespread euphemistic rationalization to "obey government" rather than God; the broader and deeper damage that resulted from the alienation of humans one from another while playing god; and the greater number of

---

46   Psalm 119:133 "Direct my footsteps according to your word; let no sin rule over me." (*NIV*)

deaths that resulted from the isolation and self-protection of the privileged than from Covid-19.

Whether the underlying reasons of my reactive and emotive anger were correct or incorrect isn't the point and either way, it wouldn't excuse sinful anger. The point at issue is, did the body of Christ as a whole stand fast while accelerated "rulers and authorities of this dark world and spiritual forces of evil"[47] came against what God enjoins? With respect to "be angry and sin not,"[48] I did not stand fast. My anger was ultimately driven by fear and/or guilt, just as all the capitulations of Christians are. The only pandemic that kills 100% of those infected with it is sin ;[49] in my case that sin manifested as anger driven by pride and ultimately, a rejection of God's sovereign purposes.

According to Romans 6:1 though, "there is therefore now no condemnation to those who are in Christ." So, for the anger, fear, and guilt that are all ultimately associated with death, and for all lesser dangers (including viruses), God in Christ is my shelter in place. To shelter with the Lord[50] is to trust God wherever led by the Spirit of God, **in Truth**. It does not mean to isolate and self-protect in a man-made house, behind a mask, or through disingenuous virtue signaling to hide self-protection in platitudes like, "it's for your safety."

---

47   Ephesians 6:12 "For our struggle is not against flesh and blood, but against the rulers, against the powers, against the world forces of this darkness, against the spiritual forces of wickedness in the heavenly places."

48   Ephesians 4:26 "Be angry, and yet do not sin; do not let the sun go down on your anger."

49   Romans 6:23 "For the wages of sin is death, but the gracious gift of God is eternal life in Christ Jesus our Lord."

50   Psalm 91:1 "One who dwells in the shelter of the Most High will lodge in the shadow of the Almighty."

CHAPTER 6

Willing and Obedient

ISIAH 1:19

*"If you are willing and obedient,
you shall eat the good of the land."*

It is common to hear Christian's deliver diatribes about the state of the nation in which they reside, or the nations in general, while actively blame-shifting. They go about killing others with their thoughts, words, and even sometimes actions, in the name of Christ. They blame many other causes for the declines they observe or hear of. That's one extreme. At the other extreme Christians respond by hiding behind intellectually infantile and preposterous conclusions about which political candidates or causes are "Christian," as if these candidates and causes will save the nation or nations from decline.

Either extreme might soothe fears and assuage guilt in individuals for a short time, but afterward the original initiators of fear and guilt fall into a memory hole just as does the personal culpability for irrational and reactive responses. Unless one self-examines they are doomed by the memory hole to reactive repetition every time a new threat looms. In reality, irrational and extreme responses to secular events never save the nation or nations, individuals, or anything else. It is prudent though, with each looming threat, to ask the question, "Is this (or any) nation "consumed because of our (**own**) iniquities ?"[51]. That question at the very least has the potential to lead one back to a consideration of Christ's willingness and obedience.

Take the United States for one example and ask whether the decline is a result of the fact that the self-identified Christians in the midst have acted like spoiled children in the blessed, miraculous anomaly of the nation's history? Is there even such a thing as a Christian nation? Or is there simply, in this case, a nation originally founded on Biblical principles that contained a large number of those with Christian values in more than name only? And has it been the case throughout history that Biblical principles lead to blessedness and that in turn, blessedness leads to pride and presumption among believers?

Is **any** nation founded in Biblical principles sustainable in a fallen world? Or by Christians looking for heaven on earth rather than Christ's return? A study of the crucifixion of Christ by Jewish religious leaders avid for an imagined heaven on earth, along with the ensuing results in the world since the resurrection of Christ, might provide some insights to answer these questions.

Is it the case that the founding of this nation and the subsequent history of blessedness contains participation in open, heinous sin such as (and not limited to) slavery, misogyny, and gross extravagance **in the name of Christ?** How long will

---

51   Isaiah 64:7 "And there is no one who calls on Your name, Who stirs himself up to take hold of You; For You have hidden Your face from us, And have consumed us because of our iniquities." (*NKJV*)

Christians hide and blame-shift rather than self-examine and repent; in this or any other nation?

Christ's body across all the earth bears the symptoms of metastatic disease that plagues all the nations. The disease among Christians is more "lusts of the flesh" and less repentance; "more lust of the eyes" and less discernment; and "more pride of life" with less humility.[52]

The symptoms of metastatic disease can be easily seen among the sacred and secular. They include but are by no means limited to more food, less nutrition; more phones, less communication; more weapons, less safety; more technology, less critical thinking; more workflows, less services; more money, less giving; more medical care, less health; more relationships, less love; more psychiatry, less sanity; more pleasure, less contentment; and more information, less wisdom. Has the body of Christ joined the "woke" nation in signaling their pet "virtues" rather than standing fast in Biblical principles?

If we aren't "eating the good of the land" is it possible we are willingly **expedient** rather than willing and **obedient**? And why? Do we care more about the good of prosperity than the fellowship of God? More about the land of the old than the New Earth? Is our hope more focused on the moment than on eternity? Certain hope, full fellowship with God's goodness, and the undying New earth are immeasurably greater—and without doubt, under the Lordship of Jesus Christ, demand obedience.

---

52   1 John 2:16 "For all that is in the world, the lust of the flesh and the lust of the eyes and the boastful pride of life, is not from the Father, but is from the world."

CHAPTER 7

Bloodless Battle

REVELATION 17:14

"They will make war on the Lamb,
and the Lamb will conquer them,
for he is Lord of lords and King of kings,
and those with Him are called and chosen and faithful."

Christ emptied Himself into the violent wreckage of human history in order to salvage some people for Himself. Until Christ returns, the nations of fallen humanity will rise and fall in a series of old and new, violent invasions. A poignant and heart-wrenching contemporary example of this violent wreckage is the legal invasion of the womb to slaughter the unborn on the altar of sexual freedom, so called.

Christ was born into that world of carnage to live as the personification of divine balance in exquisite and opposing qualities: all-embracing love joined to unyielding principle; perfect humility joined to sublime self-consciousness as God; enduring tenderness joined to omnipotent power; and self-sacrifice joined to particular devotion. People of all times and circumstances are drawn by the Spirit to Christ's exquisite influence to participate in an invasion of another kind; of His kind. Although Christ's battle was not bloodless, it was only His blood that was shed.

Restored to fellowship with God, the invasion of bloodless battle (to the extent possible)[53] includes work and prayer and giving and sharing and loving and helping and suffering and sacrifice and risk, with joy and peace and patience and kindness and the like.

As a whole, did Christians fail miserably at bloodless battle during the Covid-19 period? Was isolation and self-protection merely cowardice? Next time **you** are called to disobey something God enjoins; will **you** be the "called and chosen and faithful"? Or will you be one of the lemmings?

People don't make Jesus a King. He **is** King and they surrender all throughout life again and again; and then they call for reveille, not taps, at their funeral. Alternatively, they live like corks on the waves of the ocean, reacting and emoting again and again according to the waves of violent wreckages apart from the influence of God's goodness in Jesus Christ alone.

---

53   Romans 12:18 "If possible, so far as it depends on you, be at peace with all people." Hebrews 12:14 "Pursue peace with all people, and the holiness without which no one will see the Lord."

CHAPTER 8

Irony of Oppression

PSALM 42:11

"Why art thou cast down, O my soul?
and why disquieted within me? hope thou in God:
for I shall yet praise him,
who is the health of my countenance, and my God."

The hand of oppression will certainly increase, eventually dashing any presumptuous and near-sighted hopes for a risk-free and prosperous future in what we erroneously consider stable secular environments. The rise and fall of nations has been happening throughout history, here and there, all throughout the world ever since the fall of Adam. It will not be different for this or any other nation. Although the characteristics of rise and fall may differ the inevitability of it is a constant. In the secular environment in which I live, the United States of America, we have been careening toward a downfall for many decades.

In the rise and fall of Israel (God's initial exemplar) and in all nations throughout post Resurrection history, we can see that when God's people within a nation have been humbled by the dashing of their presumptuous or prideful hopes, the wicked don't up and go away, they oppress the righteous into becoming, by Grace, champions that overcome oppression. God's work in Christ, as well as in His forerunners and followers, illustrates this integral irony beautifully and poignantly.

If the visible Church, or Christians in particular, did not stand fast in Biblical hope while authorities played god with disease control to "keep us safe," do you suppose they'll stand fast the next time? Or do you suppose that authorities will stop playing god in order to isolate, crush, and control the influence of the one, true God?

Saul oppressed David, training him as king over God's people.[54] And by the hands of wicked men like us Christ became the champion over all the temporal and eternal oppression of all the forces of evil for all God's people of all time.[55] You might say Christ was elected to it.[56]

Perhaps God's plan includes another miraculous anomaly in which this nation (or other nations) will be restored and abundantly blessed in the principles of His Word **before** being humbled and trained by oppression. God is certainly **able** to do that. Based on His Word though, is there evidence that He will be **willing** to do that? Or that we are justified in presuming upon Him for that? Will God's love compromise by giving His people

---

54 1 Samuel 13:14 "But now your kingdom shall not endure. The Lord has sought for Himself a man after His own heart, and the Lord has appointed him ruler over His people, because you have not kept what the Lord commanded you."

55 Acts 2:23 "this Man, delivered over by the predetermined plan and foreknowledge of God, you nailed to a cross by the hands of godless men and put Him to death."

56 Matthew 28:18-20 "And Jesus came up and spoke to them, saying, "All authority in heaven and on earth has been given to Me. Go, therefore, and make disciples of all the nations, baptizing them in the name of the Father and the Son and the Holy Spirit, teaching them to follow all that I commanded you; and behold, I am with you always, to the end of the age.""

less than they need to be humbled and strengthened by the irony of oppression?

"It is finished"[57] my beloved and though we may be oppressed our lives will never become so dark that Hope cannot see light in the Promise of Deliverance in Christ alone. Do not fall into the pride of presumptuous expectations or naïve fantasies that God will give (or owes us) a life free of oppression.

---

57 John 19:30 "Therefore when Jesus had received the sour wine, He said, "It is finished!" And He bowed His head and gave up His spirit."

CHAPTER 9

Active Praise

JOB 1:20-21

*"Job got up and tore his robe and shaved his head.
Then he fell to the ground in worship and said:
"Naked I came from my mother's womb,
and naked I will depart.
The Lord gave and the Lord has taken away;*
may the name of the Lord be praised."

One moment we're filled with wonder at the works of God in creation, in history, and in our lives. And at the same time, in the old nature, we're relieved that we're living a charmed life while others suffer. The next moment we're distressed by world news, contemplation of current and historic horrors, and circumstances we face. And at the same time, in the old nature, we harbor fear that our charmed life might evaporate.

In other words, we fluctuate between a praise-filled love of life (trust and obedience) and spiritually destructive feelings and behaviors (control and expedience). What would happen if we aspired to a genuine praise-filled love of life all the time? That is, if we progressively learn to love **living** life in Christ while we're still alive, come what may? This would be instead of loving **that** we're still alive while running from the fear and guilt of death and all lesser challenges. How would this change decision making? How would it change the witness of Christ we project to those around us?

An excellent way to begin such a love of living in Christ is through the practice of active praise.[58] Active praise constructs a bridge across the chasm of the old nature and the glorious revelation of God in the all-triumphant future, confirming faith. After all, what except for faith received as a gift could cause one to exhibit a praise filled love of living during times of great pain? Even if you don't **feel** it, praise to God in spite of feelings will return one to a right state of mind.

God is worthy of praise at all times because redemption of souls comes **in and through** all circumstances, not in an immediate escape **from** all circumstances. Redemption in and through circumstances is eternal, rescue from immediate circumstances is temporary. Consequently and progressively, let us praise God at all times as we "put on the new" nature while the "old nature"[59] is being put off.

No matter the degree to which we have succeeded or failed at the obedience of praise in glorifying God before, during or since the time of Covid-19, practice will eventually end in perfection if we are united to Christ. An intentional effort toward praise is essential because greater dangers and riskier obedience are certainly in all of our futures unless of course the Lord returns.

---

58 Psalm 34:1 "I will bless the Lord at all times; His praise shall continually be in my mouth."

59 Ephesians 4:22-24 "that, in reference to your former way of life, you are to rid yourselves of the old self, which is being corrupted in accordance with the lusts of deceit, and that you are to be renewed in the spirit of your minds, and to put on the new self, which in the likeness of God has been created in righteousness and holiness of the truth."

Haven't downfall and oppression always followed mass capitulations among the disciples of Christ? And might the downfall and oppression be absolutely necessary for correcting prideful and presumptuous peoples? And is it not even more necessary for those who have lived in the context of a miraculous anomaly in civil and religious liberty? Did national, organizational, and individual capitulations begin during the period of Covid-19? If not, personally at least, will they end with it?

CHAPTER 10

Strong and Courageous

DEUTERONOMY 31:6

"Be strong and courageous.
Do not fear or be in dread of them,
for it is the Lord your God who goes with you.
He will not leave you or forsake you."

There was a mixture of the pig-headed obstinance from my old nature and some strength and courage of the new nature during the time of Covid-19 as well as at all other times of my life as a disciple of Jesus Christ. I know for sure though that control and management of disease via isolation and self-protection is not, and never will be, a Christian ideal. Assembling for worship, visiting, helping, and sheltering with the Lord **are** Christian ideals. Therefore, I decided to disobey government orders even if I did so with more pig-headedness than I ought to have had, mixed in.

When we err, do we err on God's side, trusting Christ alone for deliverance from things like pig-headed obstinance? We should do, because "He will not leave or forsake" us. **Because** He will not leave us or forsake us, it is possible to refuse to allow daily life to be defined by either fear of anything at all, or guilt about remaining sin. In other words, trusting in Christ, a person can be more and more courageously obedient while remaining sins are mixed in and progressively diminishing. Our remaining sin will be with us up until the grave. That is no excuse for collapsing like a wet noodle as opposed to standing fast in risky obedience.

Guilt feelings are **feelings** about culpability that have **already** been covered in the blood of Christ.[60] Feelings motivate reactive and emotive decisions and actions that result in the expedience of trying to manage, fix, control or atone. **Knowledge** of remaining sin and Christ's atoning work should motivate the **wisdom** of repentance, but also enervate decisions and actions in love toward God; to the obedience of trusting in Christ alone. In other words, when legitimate fear and/or guilt are discovered and recognized, it should cause us to run toward loving obedience to God, not away from love of Him in slavish fear and guilt.

During the full period of Covid-19, I assembled with like-minded individuals for corporate worship—at first in a garage and later in a church building with groups of believers that were standing fast; visited and helped, stateside and abroad, many in need from illnesses (Covid-19 included) and many from other difficulties; went on pleasure trips with like-minded people, and wherever I would otherwise have gone provided it was available and possible; wore a mask only if in deference to individuals that directly asked it of me, rather than in obedience to government order(s); crossed the state border when ordered not to; and observed the same healthy habits as I had before, during, and

---

60   1 John 1:7 "but if we walk in the Light as He Himself is in the Light, we have fellowship with one another, and the blood of Jesus His Son cleanses us from all sin."

after the Covid-19 period. If I remember correctly, I contracted Covid-19 twice. On one miraculous occasion, I did not contract Covid-19 while living unmasked and in-house with a family of six (4 young children) when they had all contracted Covid-19 at the same time.

Yes, I was pig-headed and obstinate, a personal characteristic I expect will diminish up to the grave[61] and then disappear in the completed work of Christ.[62] But I also know that I was a little bit strong and courageous, trusting in Christ alone. With God's help I'll continue in self-examination and repentance in order to lessen the pig-headed obstinance and so that I will increase in strength and courage. After all, "the path of the just [in Christ alone] is as the shining light, that shines more and more unto the perfect day" (Proverbs 4:18).

My point is that fear and guilt feelings are prohibitive to obedience and that's one of the main reasons why God says, "there is therefore now no condemnation to those in Christ." The affect and effect of sin though, will be mixed into all that we think, say, and/or do, until the Lord returns or calls us Home. That fact should not stop us from intentionally turning lovingly toward God by "taking every thought captive to the obedience of Christ."[63]

To have Christ alone is enough for any mix of remaining sin that you and I drag along with us in the process of sanctification.[64]

---

61   Hebrews 12:1b "let's rid ourselves of every obstacle and the sin which so easily entangles us, and let's run with endurance the race that is set before us."

62   Philippians 1:6 "For I am confident of this very thing, that He who began a good work among you will complete it by the day of Christ Jesus."

63   2 Corinthians 10:5 "We are destroying arguments and all arrogance raised against the knowledge of God, and we are taking every thought captive to the obedience of Christ."

64   1 Thessalonians 5:23 "Now may the God of peace Himself sanctify you entirely; and may your spirit and soul and body be kept complete, without blame at the coming of our Lord Jesus Christ."

Salvation isn't freedom from sin **now**, it is freedom from the **guilt** of sin now, and therefore from the associated fear of condemnation. The sin itself is like a plague that is cured in Christ, whose symptoms have not yet all gone[65] and which we work in love of God, to diminish.

---

65   Revelation 21:1-4 "Then I saw a new heaven and a new earth...(where) God Himself will be among them, and He will wipe away every tear from their eyes; and there will no longer be any death; there will no longer be *any* mourning, or crying, or pain...." (paraphrase)

CHAPTER 11

God is Responsible

"Yet as for me, I know that my Redeemer lives,
and at the last He will take His stand on the earth.
Even after my skin is destroyed, yet from my flesh
I will see God, Whom I, on my part, shall behold for myself,
and whom my eyes will see, and not another.
My heart faints within me!"

During the Covid-19 period, on trips to Haiti, I escaped gang violence in a boat; was surrounded by machete wielding individuals at many gang checkpoints; robbed at gunpoint; stood vulnerable and helpless on the open road twice after separately blowing out two tires; evaded being kidnapped driving through a riverbed and up a steep oxcart track; and travelled 70+ miles on a gas tank with absolutely no fuel in it. I didn't contract Covid on either trip, but I did draw conclusions about obedience to God in connection with risks.

If it isn't your time to die, nothing can kill you and if it is, nothing can keep you alive. Therefore, on any given day, in any situation, there is a 100% or 0% risk of death (or lesser harms) because God appoints the time and way[66] and our lives are in His hand.[67] Knowing this, Jesus' disciples are able to accept risks believing that God has made Himself responsible for all the consequences into which obedience leads. This is true **even** if and when, **especially** if and when, obedience leads to the first death (of the body) and there in Christ alone, we experience the full realization of having already escaped the second death.[68]

At the time I made those particular trips to Haiti, I believed it was obedient in spite of the risk to myself and my Haitian ministry partners. Since then, and at other times, I have not made trips to Haiti, even though I desired to, believing it was disobedient. It's not **what** we decide first of all, but **that** we decide **in the liberty wherewith Christ has set us free from guilt in life and fear in death.**[69]

Decisions about what to do in life, if led by fear and/or guilt, invariably end in expedient rather than obedient actions. Obedient actions are decided through study of the Word, in prayer, in realistic and sober examinations of risk, with input from others, considering God-given priorities, and not as the reactive and emotive response to fear or guilt.

Fear and guilt are the motivators of the old nature and while we **feel** them (trust me, I felt them on those trips to Haiti), we can and must intentionally set those feelings aside in order to exercise **obedient decision-making.** I heartily admit that it is a lifelong

---

66   Hebrews 9:27a "And as it is appointed unto men once to die, but after this the judgment...."

67   Psalm 31:15 "My times are in Your hand; rescue me from the hand of my enemies and from those who persecute me."

68   Revelation 21:8 "But for the cowardly, and unbelieving, and abominable, and murderers, and sexually immoral persons, and sorcerers, and idolaters, and all liars, their part will be in the lake that burns with fire and brimstone, which is the second death."

69   Galatians 5:1 "It was for freedom that Christ set us free; therefore keep standing firm and do not be subject again to a yoke of slavery."

process to do so, that it is exceedingly difficult, and that we often fail. It is, and has been, exactly that way for me. However, if feelings of fear and guilt are legitimate, they should lead to repentance and obedience, not to reactive and emotive expedience.

Take heart. There is a Redeemer regardless of what we did (or didn't) do during Covid-19 mania (or at any other time) because viruses aren't the killer and salvation isn't escape from earthly risks.

CHAPTER 12

Glorious Juxtaposition

PSALM 119:23

"Princes also sit and speak against me,
but Your servant meditates on Your statutes."

The more we stand fast, the more we exhibit the glorious juxtaposition spoken of in Psalm 119:23 between the powerful and influential forces of this world as they bloviate, and the servants of God as they simultaneously meditate. The first maintain a voluble stream of windy words while the servants of God learn to wait in the holy, quiet calm that exudes one who is in communion with God's Word on the inside. They listen intently while meditating.[70]

The powerful and influential will progressively demand more God-defying servitude than was demanded during the period of Covid-19. There is no reason to believe otherwise. Prepare for it now by practicing intense listening while simultaneously

---

70 Psalm 1:2 "But his delight is in the Law of the Lord, and on His law he meditates day and night."

meditating quietly on the inside. Learn to pause for long periods if necessary. Mull over what you hear and consider it in light of God's Word. Pray about it. What you should (or shouldn't) say or do will eventually come to you with a sense of peace that you have taken direction from God and not from princes.

Peace with God is not the initiator or the result of words and actions that are reactive and emotive. The Prince of Peace is the best and only complete example of this. Every thought, word, and deed was intentionally obedient and in complete harmony with the Father. He **felt** everything.[71] He just didn't allow those feelings to dissuade Him from obedience.

Peace (although not necessarily ease) will follow quiet meditation. Proactive and carefully measured words and actions of obedience always follow (although sometimes at length) prayer and quiet meditative communion with God. We become intentionally obedient people, not because of our feelings, but in spite of them.

Communing with God and having peace with God doesn't relieve one of the responsibilities of being involved in the lawful activities of this world, or of being obedient to authorities to the extent that God's Word and law are not violated. It can however free us from being led like lemmings into reactive and emotive actions of expedience incited by powerful and influential forces.

To answer the objection that is probably rattling around in your head, "Yes, I agree that this is an exceedingly difficult skill for all the servants of God, myself included." But still, **are** we attempting to develop the holy, quiet calm of communing with God? Do we **ever** appear to be in glorious juxtaposition to the

---

71   Hebrews 2:17 "Therefore, in things He [Christ] had to be made like His brothers [and sisters] so that He might become a merciful and faithful high priest in things pertaining to God, to make propitiation for the sins of the people."

bloviating influences of this godless world? Or are we filled with pride ourselves and incessantly bloviating; reacting and emoting to the drumbeat thrum of our own thoughts and feelings and preferences?

CHAPTER 13

The Armor

EPHESIANS 6:14-17

*"Stand firm then, with the belt of truth
buckled around your waist,
with the breastplate of righteousness in place,
and with your feet fitted with the readiness
that comes from the gospel of peace.
In addition to all this, take up the shield of faith,
with which you can extinguish all the flaming arrows
of the evil one. Take the helmet of salvation
and the sword of the Spirit, which is the word of God."*

For a full and glorious study of the armor needed to stand firm or stand fast, as enjoined by God's Word in Ephesians 6, I recommend William Gurnall's *The Christian in Complete Armour*, first published in 1662. It is a long and arduous read that is well worth the time and effort. For now though, consider the following summative statements about standing fast.[72]

---

72 Ephesians 6:13 "For this cause take unto you the whole armor of God, that ye may be able to resist in the evil day, and having finished all things, stand fast." (*GNV*)

The **belt of Truth** doesn't safeguard prosperity, physical health, or earthly opportunities. It safeguards your soul in the faith of Christ when exposed to the lies of the devil, the world, and our fallen flesh as we are being sanctified in the truth.[73]

The **breastplate of righteousness** is Christ's imputed righteousness, which frees us from the fear and guilt associated with the just condemnation of ourselves before the Holy Creator God. It also strengthens our courage in following Him, even with awareness of remaining sin and in the face of many dangers.[74]

To have our **feet fitted with the gospel of peace** isn't fashion advice. It's a reminder that wherever one goes in Christ alone, they are at peace with God.[75] When we are at peace with God, we can be certain that God will be responsible for all the circumstances into which obedience leads, especially when standing in front of His judgment throne, but also in all lesser dangers that precede that appointed time.

The **shield of faith** is a gift[76] but it isn't defense against being affected by the dark arts, of being attacked in any way, or against any other temporal danger.[77] It shields the soul from being separated from the grace of God and the love of Christ alone[78] as revealed in the Word for God's glory and our eternal good.

---

73   1 John 17:17 "Sanctify them in the truth; Your word is truth."

74   2 Corinthians 5:21 "For he hath made him to be sin for us, which knew no sin, that we should be made the righteousness of God in him."

75   Romans 5:1 "Therefore, having been justified by faith, we have peace with God through our Lord Jesus Christ."

76   Ephesians 2:8 "For by grace you have been saved through faith; and this is not of yourselves, it is the gift of God."

77   John 16:33 "These things I have spoken to you so that in Me you may have peace. In the world you have tribulation, but take courage; I have overcome the world."

78   Romans 8:38-39 "For I am convinced that neither death, nor life, nor angels, nor principalities, nor things present, nor things to come, nor powers, nor height, nor depth, nor any other created thing will be able to separate us from the love of God that is in Christ Jesus our Lord."

The **helmet of salvation** doesn't stop the mind from all reactive, emotive confusion, or from sins of omission and commission. The helmet of salvation is the framework of God's Word of Truth in the mind. If we protect our minds with the Truth about salvation, and exercise our minds with it, it protects our cogitation and meditation so that when consequent activities are chosen (or rejected) they lead toward obedience that supports a preference for the spiritual and eternal, rather than toward expedience that supports a preference for the temporal and temporary.[79]

The **sword of the Spirit** is the Word of God, which is to be used by believers at all times to nourish the soul of self and of others. The Word isn't a weapon to use against all your enemies, or the recitation of which necessarily saves you or those you are talking to. Nor is it a magic incantation. The Word has its own power[80] and does what God wills it to do in Jesus Christ. That is, God's full story will be completed for His glory and our good, through the Word that is not only in phonemic symbols but through Jesus Christ, that Word made flesh. You and I only have to be prepared[81] to study it, believe it, know it and speak it fitly,[82] in love.[83] God will do with His Word, what He will do. You? Simply be obedient.

---

79   Colossians 3:1-4 "Therefore, if you have been raised with Christ, keep seeking the things that are above, where Christ is, seated at the right hand of God. Set your minds on the things *that are* above, not on the things that are on earth. For you have died, and your life is hidden with Christ in God. When Christ, who is our life, is revealed, then you also will be revealed with Him in glory."

80   Hebrews 4:12 "For the word of God is living and active, and sharper than any two-edged sword, even penetrating as far as the division of soul and spirit, of both joints and marrow, and able to judge the thoughts and intentions of the heart."

81   2 Timothy 4:2 "preach the word; be ready in season and out of season; correct rebuke, and exhort, with great patience and instruction."

82   Proverbs 25:11 "A word fitly spoken is like apples of gold in pictures of silver."

83   Ephesians 4:15 "but speaking the truth in love, we are to grow up in all aspects into Him who is the head, that is, Christ."

Christ's Kingdom will fully come, and His will be fully done when He returns to judge the world and usher in the New Heaven and Earth.[84] In the meantime my dearly beloved sons and daughters, "…be firm, immovable, always excelling in the work of the Lord, knowing that your labor is not in vain in the Lord" (1 Corinthians 15:58). Stand fast until you've been called all the way Home.

---

*"Now to Him who is able to keep you from stumbling, and to make you **stand** in the presence of His glory blameless with great joy, to the only God our Savior, through Jesus Christ our Lord, be glory, majesty, dominion and authority, before all time and now and forever.*
Amen
(JUDE 1:23, 24)."

---

84 Revelation 21:1 "Then I saw a new heaven and a new earth; for the first heaven and the first earth passed away, and there is no longer any sea."

CHAPTER 14

Heart of Re-formation

HOSEA 4:1

"Hear the Word of the Lord, O children of Israel,
for the Lord has a controversy
with the inhabitants of the land.
There is no faithfulness or steadfast love,
and no knowledge of God in the land."

"There is nothing new under the sun."[85]

New dangers that arise are unpredictable and worthy of extensive study. I'm not suggesting that Covid-19 wasn't a new danger, but that dangers aren't new under the sun. Covid-19 should have and does warrant serious study on the part of those qualified to do so, with all the resources and knowledge God has provided. I **am** suggesting that the powers of darkness successfully

---

85 Ecclesiastes 1:9 "What has been, it is what will be, and what has been done, it is what will be done. So there is nothing new under the sun."

used Covid-19 as an opportunity to further isolate, crush and control civil, and more importantly, religious liberty. On the whole where God enjoins one thing, Christians did the opposite in response to authoritative orders. This is **especially** grievous in the land blessed by civil and religious liberty and founded on Biblical principles. On the whole institutions and individuals that self-identified as Christian contributed more to the decline rather than the preservation of Truth among the nations during Covid-19.

People die sad, unexpected deaths and suffer with disease symptoms while living. I'm not suggesting that the possibility of death during Covid-19 should not have saddened and concerned us, that some suffered with more severe symptoms than others, or that anyone should have been reckless with their own health or the health of others. But let's be clear death, symptoms, and the need for responsible self-care are not new under the sun. I am also not suggesting that those people with individual, known vulnerabilities should not have taken extra care to preserve the life God gave them. I **am** suggesting that Christians should do what God enjoins while taking reasonable measures with their health, and not by merely running from illness and death in isolation and self-protection. Instead they should run toward the work God has given them to do, trusting Him.

Sometimes the body of Christ capitulates. Capitulation of Christ followers, Old and New testament, is not new under the sun. Although many or most contemporary scientists, and much of the world population, believe **in** science and scientists as the god(s) that will eventually eliminate the effects of the fall, including death, it isn't so. Scientists and authorities were **playing** god during Covid-19, and those who "believe in science" played along as their disciples. That is also not new under the sun. The problem, and my objection, is that leaders and followers of Christ within Christendom, on the whole, also played along. Even though the body of Christ sometimes capitulates, it's **also** not new under the sun that after capitulation we can stand up and stand fast for Jesus. It's never too late to do it again and again.

Feelings of fear and guilt will always be mixed in. I'm not suggesting that we ignore feelings of fear and guilt as a reality that impacts our decisions and actions but let's face it, fear and guilt are not new under the sun. I'm suggesting that we self-examine, and then set fear and guilt aside as the **motivators** of our decisions and actions. Courage is the realization of fear and guilt while acting simultaneously in support of that which is more important than fear or guilt, because Christ alone is enough, and nothing is more important. For legitimate fear and guilt, discovered through self-examination, run to Christ alone. The Bible gives many instructions for that; react and emote with expedience are not among those instructions.

Christians, on the whole and as individuals, struggle with obedience versus expedience because the powers of darkness are always at work, and Christians carry remaining sin to the grave. Again, that is not new under the sun. The heart of reformation is to be **re-formed** in newness of life,[86] over and over and over toward the likeness of Christ.[87] Whether you collapsed like a wet noodle or stood fast during Covid-19 (or in any other challenges of life) it is never too late to stand up and stand fast for

---

86   Romans 6:4 "Therefore we have been buried with Him through baptism into death, so that, just as Christ was raised from the dead through the glory of the Father, so we too may walk in newness of life."

87   2 Corinthians 3:18 "But we all, with open face beholding as in a glass the glory of the Lord, are changed into the same image from glory to glory, even as by the Spirit of the Lord." (*KJV*)

Jesus; again and again and again: I know for sure that I have had to do so.

Obey what God enjoins through freedom in Christ, against any efforts to isolate, crush, and control the liberties that afford a free expression of the Gospel. Take shelter under the wings of the Almighty,[88] confident that God is responsible for all the consequences of obedience and there is no condemnation to those that are in Christ.

"Come now" my dear ones, "let us reason together." Even "though your sins are like scarlet, they shall be as white as snow."[89] After all, "you were bought with a price." I urge you not to "become servants of men."[90] Instead, seek the Kingdom of Jesus Christ and His righteousness one day at a time in daily re-formation. Yesterday is past and tomorrow's worries will take care of themselves. "Sufficient unto the day is the evil thereof."[91]

---

88   Psalm 91:4 "He will cover you with His pinions and under His wings you may take refuge; His faithfulness is a shield and a wall."

89   Isaiah 1:18 "Come now, and let us reason together," Says the Lord, "Though your sins are like scarlet, They shall be as white as snow; Though they are red like crimson, They shall be as wool." (NKJV)

90   1 Corinthians 7:23 "Ye are bought with a price; be not ye the servants of men."

91   Matthew 6:33-34 "But seek ye first the kingdom of God, and his righteousness; and all these things shall be added unto you. Take therefore no thought for the morrow: for the morrow shall take thought for the things of itself. Sufficient unto the day is the evil thereof." (KJV)

WORKS CITED

Dawkins, R. (1976). *The Selfish Gene*. Oxford University Press.

Dawkins, R. (2006). *The God Delusion*. United Kingdom: Bantam Press.

Dawkins, R. (2006). *The God Delusion*. United Kingdom: Bantam Press.

Dylan, B. (1979, May). *Gotta Serve Somebody* [Recorded by B. Dylan]. Sheffield, Alabama.

Foxe, J. (1978). *Foxe's Book of Martyrs*. Grand Rapids, MI: Baker Book House.

Roberts, A. (1980, April 4). *The Plague in England*. Retrieved from historytoday.com: https://www.historytoday.com/archive/feature/plague-england

The Spurgeon Center for Biblical Preaching at Midwestern Seminary. (2020, March 3). *Spurgeon and the Cholera Outbreak of 1854*. Retrieved from spurgeon.org: https://www.spurgeon.org/resource-library/blog-entries/spurgeon-and-the-cholera-outbreak-of-1854/

www.ingramcontent.com/pod-product-compliance
Lightning Source LLC
Chambersburg PA
CBHW022040090426
42741CB00007B/1144